HI I'M SAL

I love finding out how people used to live. I wish I could go back in time and have dinner at Chedworth. Eating while lazing on sofas sounds like fun!

YOU CAN FIND OUT MORE ABOUT DINNERTIME IN ROMAN BRITAIN ON PAGE 12.

HI I'M ASH

I love taking things apart to find out how they work. Did you know that the Romans installed underfloor heating at Chedworth?

YOU CAN FIND OUT HOW IT WORKED ON PAGE 22.

 SNAIL TALES

Chedworth is home to rare Roman snails. Keep an eye out for its star snail, Felix the Helix – he's full of interesting facts!

 GET INVOLVED

There are lots of fun things to do, from puzzles and quizzes to making your own mosaics.

 LOOK FOR CLUES

Archaeologists look for evidence to help them find out about the past. You'll see this sign in the guidebook when a clue from Chedworth tells us more about life in Roman Britain.

WELCOME TO BRITANNIA

Before the Romans came, Britain was inhabited by tribes known to us as Celts. The Celts were fierce warriors. They were also good at farming and created beautiful art. The Romans had been trading with British tribes for years before they marched in with an army. Once they'd invaded, the Roman army stayed for more than 350 years.

AD

60/61
In the east, tribal queen Boudicca leads a rebellion against the Romans. She sets fire to the cities of Colchester, London and St Albans, and slaughters their inhabitants, but soon the Romans strike back and win.

55BC & 54BC
Julius Caesar makes two attempts at invading Britain, and is unsuccessful both times!

2ND CENTURY
AN EARLY VERSION OF THE VILLA AT CHEDWORTH IS BUILT.

122
Emperor Hadrian builds a wall right across Britain to defend the edge of the Empire.

AD43
The Emperor Claudius invades Britain. This time the Romans aren't messing about. Claudius' army of 40,000 soldiers sweeps across the south-east of Britain.

70-84
The Romans conquer what is now Wales, northern England and Lowland Scotland. Governor Agricola persuades British leaders to speak, dress and act more like Romans.

BC

4TH CENTURY

THE 'GOLDEN AGE' OF ROMAN BRITAIN, AND A VILLA BUILDING BOOM. AT CHEDWORTH, THEY MAKE THE VILLA LARGER AND GET THE DECORATORS IN.

212

Everyone living permanently in the Roman Empire is now officially a Roman citizen (apart from slaves!). *Hail Caesar!*

367

Britain is under attack by foreign tribes – the Angles, the Saxons and the Jutes.

410

The End of Roman Britain

British leaders ask the Emperor to protect them against foreign attacks, but he writes back saying that they will have to take care of it themselves. Britain is no longer truly part of the Roman Empire. Foreign tribes move in and towns and villas gradually crumble into ruins. Trees grow up through mosaic floors and soil gradually buries the buildings.

1864

THE VILLA AT CHEDWORTH IS DISCOVERED AND EXCAVATED BY ANTIQUARIANS.

313

Emperor Constantine 'the Great' makes Christianity legal.

400

THE EMPIRE IS WEAKENED BY CIVIL WAR AND UNDER THREAT. AROUND THIS TIME, THE VILLA AT CHEDWORTH LOSES ITS LUXURIOUS SHEEN. SOME OF THE BUILDINGS CONTINUE TO BE USED FOR FARMING.

1924

Chedworth Roman Villa is placed in the hands of the National Trust to preserve it for people in the future (like you!).

ALL ROMAN EMPERORS WERE KNOWN AS CAESAR.

Nobody knows the Roman name, so we call it Chedworth Roman Villa. What would you call it?

THE A429, WHICH RUNS NEAR THE VILLA TODAY, WAS BUILT ON THE REMAINS OF THE FOSSE WAY.

CHEDWORTH: GATEWAY TO THE WORLD!

Chedworth Roman Villa was a luxury home set in peaceful countryside. It was close to the city of Cirencester, the second largest city in Roman Britain, and the army's fort at Gloucester. Just a short horse-ride away was the Fosse Way, a major highway which ran all the way from Lincoln to Exeter. It formed part of a vast network of roads built by the Romans which connected London (Londinium) to Orléans (Cenabum) in France and to Rome (Roma) in Italy.

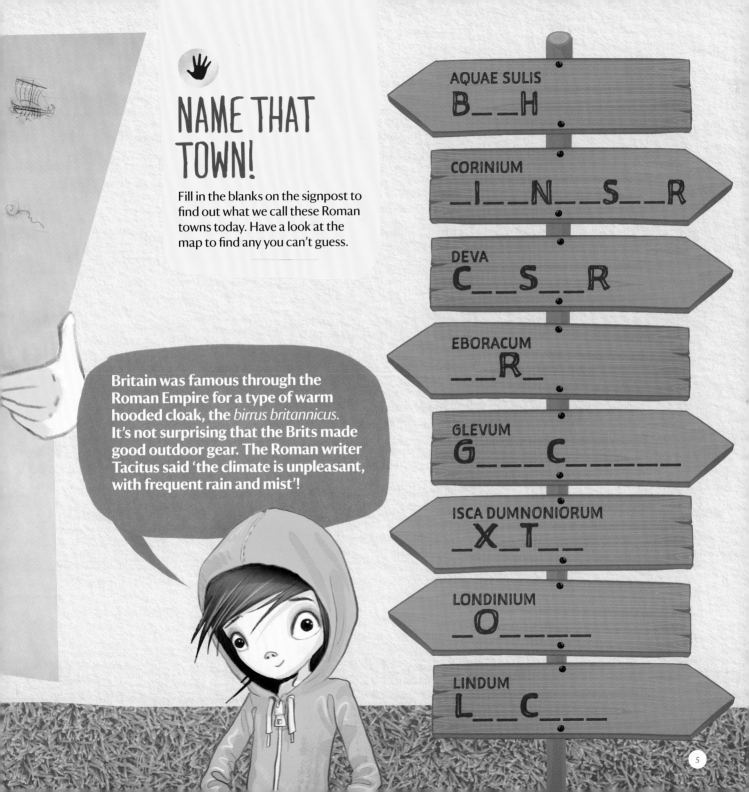

NAME THAT TOWN!

Fill in the blanks on the signpost to find out what we call these Roman towns today. Have a look at the map to find any you can't guess.

Britain was famous through the Roman Empire for a type of warm hooded cloak, the *birrus britannicus*. It's not surprising that the Brits made good outdoor gear. The Roman writer Tacitus said 'the climate is unpleasant, with frequent rain and mist'!

AQUAE SULIS
B _ _ H

CORINIUM
_ I _ _ N _ _ _ S _ _ R

DEVA
C _ _ _ S _ _ _ R

EBORACUM
_ _ R _

GLEVUM
G _ _ _ _ C _ _ _ _ _ _

ISCA DUMNONIORUM
_ X _ T _ _

LONDINIUM
_ O _ _ _ _

LINDUM
L _ _ C _ _ _

WHAT DO ARCHAEOLOGISTS DO?

Archaeology uncovers new clues from the past. For example, on a recent dig at Chedworth archaeologists discovered a new grand room near the North Baths as well as some more hidden mosaics which meant the site maps had to be **redrawn**.

There are more Roman remains waiting to be discovered all around the country. Each dig can teach us something new about the Romans.

MODERN ARCHAEOLOGISTS:

- keep notes on where every find comes from, including how deep underground it was

- publish what they find so other people know what's been done

- use the information they have gathered to work out what order things were built in, and how their use might have changed over time

- use modern technology like GPS and geophysical surveying which creates maps of archaeological features below the surface of the ground

RABBIT ARCHAEOLOGISTS

In the early 1860s, a gamekeeper in Gloucestershire, who was digging a stuck ferret out of a rabbit warren in some woods, spotted strange coloured cubes. They were bits of Roman tile, and a while later a mosaic started to appear.

Thanks to the ferret and the rabbits he had discovered the remains of Chedworth Roman Villa, which had been lying underground for hundreds of years.

'It was a lovely surprise when we uncovered the new mosaics in the north wing. We would like to find out more by doing more digs at Chedworth, but we only have enough time and funding for two weeks a year.'

Lorna Hetherington
House & Monument Steward
Chedworth Roman Villa

This is John Scott, 3rd Earl of Eldon. He owned the land when the Roman remains were first discovered. It was his uncle, James Farrer, who arranged the excavation of the villa in 1864.

MEET FRED

Fred Norman was 15 in 1864 when he helped on the archaeological dig at Chedworth. Word soon got around that something exciting was happening, and the crowds of people who came to look started getting in the way. People were damaging the mosaics, poking them with umbrellas and sticks, and it was one of Fred's jobs to stop them. 'Thousands came while we were working on the Villa for about three years,' he said. More than 60 years later, Fred still remembered how exciting it was, 'we thought it was wonderful seeing these little stones'.

VICTORIAN ANTIQUARIANS:

- moved the finds around and didn't keep notes of where exactly they'd been found

- wrote only about the things they thought were interesting

- kept the mosaics where they were and covered some of them with viewing huts

- built a museum at Chedworth to show off some of the objects that were found

THE WORD 'ARCHAEOLOGY' COMES FROM THE GREEK FOR 'THE STUDY OF ANCIENT THINGS'.

A villa was a grand Roman country house with farmland around it. About a thousand Roman villas have been found in Britain, most of which are hidden underground now. The most crowded hotspots for villas were in southern England, and there were plenty in the area around Chedworth. Villas were designed to be impressive, and its combination of exceptional size, baths, mosaics and central heating put Chedworth in the premier league.

MEANWHILE, EVERYWHERE ELSE....

Only a few lucky people in Roman Britain lived in villas. In the towns, expensive houses had several rooms and mosaics, while poor families might live in one room above a shop. Many people, however, still lived in the same sort of houses Britain had been full of before the Romans came. They were wooden, had thatched roofs and were round – no fancy Roman corners here! These round houses weren't always basic, and some even had a porch over the entrance and separate storage and sleeping areas.

CLOSED FOR RENOVATIONS – AGAIN

Like most Roman villas, Chedworth was always being renovated and extended. Archaeologists look at how the walls fit together to get a rough idea of when different parts were built. From about the year AD150 there were a few small buildings, and then around the year 300 someone joined them up into the villa's rough shape now. Around 350, the owners added more rooms, new baths, a toilet block, and mosaics including Chedworth's star feature, the floor of the dining room. Rich people across southern Britain were in the middle of a craze for luxury Roman villas at this time. By 400, the boom was over.

WHAT IS A VILLA?

CHEDWORTH:
THE LAP OF LUXURY

This world-class property boasts TWO bath-houses, bespoke mosaic floors, and all the latest technology including state-of-the-art hypocaust central heating, running water, and multi-seat toilet. Nestled in a valley with stunning views, the sloping site makes your guests walk uphill to your imposing home, climbing to the inner courtyard where you can greet the most favoured VIPs in style. Handy for Cirencester, Gloucester and the Fosse Way. **Be the envy of the other 99%. Live the high life at Chedworth!**

✋ WORDSEARCH

You might find all these things around a Roman villa – and in this wordsearch.

BATH · COURTYARD · SNAIL
VILLA · HYPOCAUST · TOILET
MOSAIC · SPRING · ROMANS

M	B	E	L	V	O	M	R	E	I
E	A	L	L	I	V	O	M	D	P
S	T	R	M	D	O	S	R	S	U
P	H	Y	P	O	C	A	U	S	T
R	V	L	O	M	Y	I	T	R	S
I	I	T	A	T	A	C	S	M	E
N	T	C	R	O	M	A	N	S	O
G	A	U	E	N	S	L	A	E	C
L	O	T	E	T	V	L	I	U	P
C	M	U	Y	T	O	I	L	E	T

WHO LIVED AT CHEDWORTH?

ROMAN OR BRITISH?

We think that the family who lived at Chedworth were probably Romano-British, meaning they were from British families, and were Roman citizens. The evidence found by archaeologists at Chedworth shows that they ate Roman food, worshipped Roman gods, washed in Roman-style baths, and used Roman money.

🔍 MONEY TALKS

Someone dropped this coin at Chedworth Roman Villa. It is a silver coin of Julian II who was Emperor from AD360–3. This proves that people must have been at the villa at some point during this period. Coins like this can be crucial for helping archaeologists put together the story of a site.

RICH OR POOR?

The family at Chedworth must have been among the richest people for miles around. The head of the family might have been a landowner, or even a government official.

At Chedworth, there were lots of dirty jobs that needed to be done, like cleaning the baths and toilets, looking after the farm animals and stoking the fires. These smelly jobs would have been done by servants, or possibly by slaves.

MEET THE FAMILY

In Roman families, the husband, or the oldest male in the house, known as the *paterfamilias*, was in charge of the household, as well as all of the servants and slaves who worked for them. His wife's job description included running the house, having babies, and also looking elegant in order to bring honour to the family. The children at Chedworth probably had a teacher at home while they were young. Once the boys were old enough they would have gone to school to learn all the Latin and Greek literature a true Roman was expected to be able to quote.

LOOSE HAIR – ONLY OLDER MARRIED WOMEN WORE THEIR HAIR UP IN COMPLICATED STYLES.

HOOD CLOAK

NECKLACE MADE OF AMBER BEADS

BELT

LONG WOOLLEN TUNIC WITH SLEEVES

LEATHER SANDALS

BULLA – A MAGICAL CHARM AGAINST EVIL SPIRITS, GIVEN TO A NEW BABY AND WORN UNTIL A BOY TURNED 16 OR A GIRL GOT MARRIED.

SHORTER TUNIC

NARROW TROUSERS FOR COLD WEATHER

✋ COLOURING

The Romans loved decoration and the children of Chedworth were rich, so make it colourful!

A CHEDWORTH DINNER PARTY

Lucky guests invited to *cena* (dinner) at Chedworth were treated to a lavish feast, as their hosts showed off their money and style.

Roman table manners didn't always include sitting up properly. Instead, people lay sideways on couches on three sides of a table set in the middle. By the 4th century, the villa might have had chairs instead, but dinner was served the same way, gourmet dishes were set on the table on silver or glass plates, and the diners helped themselves with fancy spoons. A dinner party also needed lots of servants including cooks in the kitchen, waiters to bring in all the different courses, and musicians to create the right atmosphere.

We know which room at Chedworth was the dining room because of the mosaic on the floor. Roman dining rooms had two different parts. Half of the floor was patterned where the diners sat, and the other half had pictures for everyone to admire while they ate and chatted. This space might also have been used for entertainers during really grand meals.

BE OUR GUEST!

A villa like Chedworth was a party venue as well as a home. Romans knew how to have fun, and rich people liked to show their guests an expensively good time.

WOULD YOU BE BRAVE ENOUGH TO TRY GARUM?

🔍 FOREIGN FOOD

Romans stored all sorts of things, from wine to wheat, in long pots called *amphorae*. Pieces of amphora that came from Spain and Italy have been found at Chedworth, showing that people in Britain were eating food from many hundreds of miles away.

SHOPPING LIST

The kitchen servants at Chedworth have made a list of some of the delicious food they need for a weekend of parties:

- WINE (IMPORTED FROM EUROPE)
- OLIVES
- CHICKEN
- WILD BOAR
- OYSTERS
- FISH
- GARUM*
- GARLIC
- GINGER
- ASPARAGUS
- BREAD
- CHERRIES
- GRAPES

*STRONG ROMAN SAUCE MADE FROM ROTTEN FISH

HAVING FUN

Once they'd eaten all they could, there were lots of fun activities on offer for villa guests. Hunting on horseback for wild boar or deer was popular with rich Romans, or they could go to Cirencester to see a gladiator fight in the arena in there. Chariot races were sometimes held in Britain too. Graffiti from Chedworth seems to show that someone there was a fan of the famous chariot racing team called the 'Greens'. The young children would have played with dolls, balls, kites, and other toys.

THE ROMAN WORD FOR DINING ROOM IS *TRICLINIUM*. IT COMES FROM THE GREEK WORDS FOR 'THREE COUCHES'.

WHAT'S FOR SUPPER?

While the VIP diners in a villa were nibbling on baked dormice and honey cakes, and sipping foreign wine, the ordinary locals made do with vegetable stew, porridge, and bread, with the odd bit of meat on special occasions. Pork was especially popular, and the rich also ate game, such as wild boar hunted on their own estates.

🔍 KITCHEN KIT

This piece of pottery is smooth on one side but has pieces of grit stuck on the other. It was part of a bowl called a *mortarium*, and the gritty inside was used for grinding up ingredients. Cooking pots, knives, and spoons have been found at Chedworth, and we're even sure which room was the main kitchen – you can still see the bottom of the oven.

> In towns, you didn't have to eat at home. People who didn't have their own kitchen could pop into a takeaway shop and pick up a *farinata*, a stuffed pancake.

1

5

8

9

TASTY CROSSWORD

ACROSS

1. ____ boar, a pig that lives in the woods **(4)**
2. Furniture to put your food on **(5)**
5. Salt and _____, a spice the Romans brought to Britain **(6)**
7. Special dish for grinding ingredients **(9)**
8. Smelly sauce made from fish **(5)**
9. Alcoholic grape drink **(4)**
10. ____ oil, useful for cooking and dressing salads **(5)**

DOWN

3. Small sleepy mammal, baked as a Roman delicacy **(8)**
4. Needed to make toast **(5)**
6. Room where you cook **(7)**

GET CREATIVE

Romans loved to decorate floors with mosaics – pictures and patterns made up of small cubes of stone, tile or glass. Hundreds of Roman mosaic floors have been found in Britain, but the number of high-quality mosaics at Chedworth show us that the villa was special.

Here's one of the stars of the famous Chedworth dining room mosaic: Winter. We know he's supposed to be Winter because he's wrapped up in a *birrus britannicus*, and also because he's holding a dead branch and a dead hare – ready to be made into a nice warm stew, maybe?

MOSAIC CARE

Roman mosaics are fragile. Once it's been uncovered, a mosaic needs to be carefully looked after. At Chedworth, all the mosaics were left where they were, rather than being moved to a museum. Some were covered with buildings to protect them from the weather. The rest were recorded and then buried again to keep them safe. You may be able to see them on a visit to Chedworth in the future if more cover buildings are put up.

Dust and dirt fall onto the mosaic from people standing on the walkways above, so the floors at Chedworth have to be swept each week. Too much dust would not only prevent people from seeing the patterns and colours, but could also provide somewhere for moss or lichen to grow.

Each year the team does a deep clean. They use soft brushes first, then loosen harder crusts of dirt with bamboo sticks. Special rubber 'smoke sponges' collect small pieces of debris. Lastly, they wipe down the mosaics using a sponge and pure deionised water (chemicals in tap water could get into the tiles).

Damp conditions also harm mosaics, and encourage algae to grow – the same stuff that makes ponds go green and slimy. So the Chedworth team kills the algae using lamps that give out sterilising ultraviolet light.

🔍 LOOK UP!

Mosaics were only the start of a villa's interior decoration. The walls and ceilings would have been just as showy, or maybe more so. Archaeologists at Chedworth found these colourful pieces of painted plaster. Like houses elsewhere in the Empire, villas in Britain must have been full of bright wall paintings, with clashing colours and patterns. Add in lots of carved stone statues and wooden furniture, and you get a 'look' that's anything but minimalist.

✋ COULD YOU BE A MOSAIC MASTER?

✓ If you're feeling inspired by Chedworth's mosaics, try making your own.

✓ Start by choosing a repeating border for the edge of the mosaic. Copy one of these examples, or design your own.

✓ Next, lightly draw a picture in the middle – Romans especially liked pictures of gods and animals. Don't make it too detailed.

✓ Finally, colour in whole squares one at a time to turn your picture into a mosaic fit for a villa!

Instead of colouring in your squares, you could cut up an old colourful magazine into lots of small squares, and then stick then onto your design using craft glue to build up the picture.

HERE'S HOW A ROMAN MASTER MOSAIC MAKER WOULD HAVE DONE IT:

1. gathered different coloured stones, clay tiles and glass

2. broke them up carefully into small cubes

3. spread a layer of mortar on the floor

4. following the design the buyer ordered, pushed the tiles into the mortar until only the tops showed

5. left the mortar to dry

6. polished the mosaic and presented it to the happy customer

IT'S BATH TIME....

ON OFFER AT THE PUBLIC BATHS

- HAIRCUTS IN THE LATEST ROMAN STYLES
- MANICURES
- BODY HAIR PLUCKED
- REVIVING MASSAGES
- STUBBORN EARWAX REMOVED
- SPACE FOR WORKING OUT
- DELICIOUS SNACKS

Baths were extremely important to the Romans. They took their famous way of bathing with them all across the Empire, including to Britain. Anyone who wanted to look, smell and feel more like a civilised Roman would need to start by having a bath!

... AND TIME FOR A GOSSIP

Instead of using private bathrooms like we do today, Roman towns and military forts had big public baths where everyone washed together, though men and women may have bathed separately, The baths were social places, where you met your friends, gossiped, exercised, and played games.

BATH TIME AT CHEDWORTH

Ordinary homes in Roman Britain wouldn't have had their own bathrooms, but Chedworth was such a grand villa that it had two heated bath houses, complete with intricate mosaic floors.

Chedworth's West Baths were a series of rooms, heated to different temperatures. Use your imagination to explore them and have a true Roman bath experience:

APODYTERIUM: the changing room, where you'd leave your clothes.

TEPIDARIUM: the warm room. Try rubbing olive oil into your skin – it helps clean off the dirt.

CALDARIUM: the hottest room, with a hot-water pool and clouds of steam to get the sweat pouring. Use a metal tool called a strigil to scrape off the soggy mix of dirt, oil and dead skin you're now covered with.

FRIGIDARIUM: the cold room. It's easy to remember the name, just think of a fridge. There's a cold pool to jump into if you're feeling brave.

A CLOSE LOOK

Archaeologists studying the walls at Chedworth discovered that the North Bath House we can see today is actually built on top of an earlier set of baths. These early baths date from the second century, and were used for 200 years before being replaced when a new set of baths in the West Range were built.

As they no longer needed the northern baths, the owners built on top of them and turned them into a *laconicum*, a sauna-like bath using dry heat instead of steam. This was named after a place called Laconia, where the famously tough Spartan people lived – you had to be strong to stand the heat!

A.

B.

C.

D.

E.

F.

G.

PACK YOUR WASH KIT FOR A ROMAN BATH!

Which of these things should you **NOT** take in for your dip at Chedworth?

A – SPONGE ON A STICK

B – STRIGIL (A METAL SKIN SCRAPER)

C – OILS

D – SOAP

E – SWIMMING COSTUME

F – EAR WAX REMOVER

G – TWEEZERS (FOR PLUCKING OUT BODY HAIR)

Do you think a Roman bath would leave you cleaner than your bath at home?

It could take the slaves at Chedworth <u>THREE DAYS</u> to heat up the baths by stoking the fires with wood!

BRILLIANT BUILDERS

From running water to concrete, the Romans brought lots of ingenious ideas and new technology to Britain.

This is a hypocaust, a Roman underfloor heating system. The floor is raised up on *pilae* (pillars) made of tiles, so that air can circulate around. A fire at one end of the hypocaust heats the air, and the vents in the walls on the far side draw the hot air through the space and let it escape through the roof. The hot air heats the *pilae* which heat the floor above.

AT CHEDWORTH, SOME OF THE PILLARS HAVE TO BE WRAPPED UP IN WARM 'SOCKS' BEFORE THE WINTER, OTHERWISE FREEZING AND MELTING WATER WOULD CAUSE CRACKS.

WATER WORKS

The Romans were experts in moving water around. They liked to build villas where water was already available – Chedworth has a natural spring – but in other places they diverted rivers and even built bridges known as aqueducts to bring fresh water into their towns. They laid underground pipes to carry water around their cities and homes. At Chedworth you can see some of its original lead pipes in the museum.

> Our word 'plumbing' comes from *plumbum*, **Latin for lead,** the metal Romans used to make water pipes and cooking pots.

SHARED SEATS

A small room next to the main kitchen at Chedworth had a sewer and clean running water, which drained out in a channel along the floor. This plumbing, together with a stone base for wooden seats, tells us that this room was the *latrina* (toilet). The channel in the floor would be used to clean the shared sponges on sticks which people used instead of toilet paper and the running water would have 'flushed' the waste away. Before the Romans the smelly waste would have just sat at the bottom of a pit – phewey!. The seat would have had several holes so that more than one person could go at the same time – but there were no cubicles! Roman loos were a place to chat.

BUILDING A NEW WORLD

To the British, who had been living in wooden round houses. Roman builders must have seemed futuristic. They built solid, straight roads all across the country using layers of different sized stones; used arches to make big buildings stronger; and even built with concrete!

THE NYMPHAEUM

The villa at Chedworth was built near a natural spring, which was probably a holy place for the local Celtic tribe. The Celts worshipped nature, and their sacred places were usually around springs, rivers, or groups of trees. The Romans called their nature spirits who lived in water 'nymphs', which is why we call the sacred spring at Chedworth the 'nymphaeum'. The people who lived in the villa built an octagonal pool to collect the spring water before piping it around. They built a shrine where they could pray that their good luck, and their water, wouldn't run out.

There are signs of other local gods at Chedworth, like statues that seem to represent a *lar* (a household spirit) and a *genius loci* (the spirit of a particular place).

CELTIC SHRINE

NYMPHAEUM

WHAT WOULD YOUR HOUSEHOLD GOD LOOK LIKE?

WHO DID THEY WORSHIP?

Local British people had worshipped many gods for as far back as we know, and the Romans brought even more with them. There were the three most powerful gods, Jupiter, Juno and Minerva; and other gods for almost every occasions, like Mars, god of war; Venus, goddess of love; Diana, goddess of hunting, and many, many more ....

ADOPT A GOD

When it came to gods, most Romans thought you could never have too many. Wherever they went, they found new religions. Shrines to the Egyptian goddess Isis and the Persian bull-slaying god Mithras have been found in Britain, as these exotic gods were popular with soldiers and traders. When they got to Britain, the Romans would match the Celtic gods they found there with a similar Roman god. So Sulis, a powerful Celtic goddess, became Sulis Minerva, and the war god Camulos was matched up with the Roman war god Mars to become Mars Camulos.

THIS LITTLE CARVING FROM CHEDWORTH SHOWS THE GOD MARS LENUS. HE'S ORIGINALLY FROM GERMANY, AND HE'S OFTEN LINKED TO HUNTING.

A USEFUL STONE

This little carving is a Christian symbol called a chi-rho, the first two letters of 'Christ' in the Greek alphabet. It was carved into a stone from the edge of the pool in Chedworth's nymphaeum. This carving shows Christianity must have been in fashion at the villa, probably in the 300s when Emperor Constantine started supporting the new religion. But later on, this stone with its holy sign was taken away from the nymphaeum and recycled as an ordinary building block. It suggests that people at Chedworth, like elsewhere in the Empire, became Christian and then went back to worshipping other gods.

TRANSLATORS REQUIRED?

Before the Romans invaded, people in Britain spoke versions of Celtic. They didn't use writing, but we know some of their language from old place names and from studying modern languages that come from Celtic, like Welsh and Gaelic. After the invasion, Latin became very useful for talking to the new people in charge. Traders and people in towns spoke Latin, and so did the British leaders, but in the countryside ordinary people probably carried on speaking Celtic. Rich people who lived in villas like Chedworth spoke excellent Latin and would also have learned ancient Greek, like other well-educated Romans.

X OUT OF X

Romans didn't have the same numbers we use today. Instead they used letters, in a system now called Roman numerals.

HERE'S HOW IT WORKS:

1 - i
2 - ii
3 - iii
4 - iv (one before five)
5 - v
6 - vi (one after five)
7 - vii
8 - viii
9 - ix (one before ten)
10 - x
20 - xx ; 30- xxx ;
50 - L ; 100 - C ;
500 - D ; 1000 - M
(used more today than by the Romans)

WRITING

The Romans brought writing to Britain, where people found lots of uses for it. They wrote about dead people on tombstones; they wrote on altars, to thank the gods for helping out; they scribbled on walls; and soldiers wrote home to ask for more socks and pants. Some people used the power of writing to carve **curses** on flattened lead. One 'curse tablet' said that whoever stole the writer's cloak wouldn't be able to sleep or have children until they gave it back!

TRY A FEW DIFFERENT NUMBERS FOR PRACTICE, THEN ANSWER THESE QUESTIONS:

1. How old are you?

2. How many snails can you count on this page?

3. When was the villa at Chedworth discovered?

DO YOU SPEAK LATIN?

Latin was still used in parts of Europe after the end of the Roman Empire, such as France, and came back to Britain later on in different forms. So there are lots of English words with Latin roots. This means you might understand more Latin than you think.

See if you can guess what these Latin words mean and match them to the right pictures.

A. CANDELA
B. ROSA
C. CASEUS
D. ELEPHANTUS
E. FAMILIA
F. NASUS
G. BRITANNIA

LATIN ON THE MAP

If you look on a map of Britain you'll find lots of place names ending in 'chester', 'caster' or 'cester' – like Cirencester or Manchester. The Latin word for an army camp was *castra*, so place names like this usually tell you that there had been a Roman military base nearby.

LEARN LATIN – GO TO WALES!

Language in Britain changed a lot after the Romans left, and people in England soon picked up the Germanic language of the North European tribes who had moved in, which slowly developed into modern English. The many English words with Latin roots were mostly introduced into the language long after the Romans had gone. But another British language is still using hundreds of words the Romans really did leave behind: Welsh.

Latin	Welsh	English
mare	mor	sea
fenestra	ffenestr	window
medicus	meddyg	doctor

WITHINGTON 1½
CHELTENHAM 8½

ROMAN VILLA 1
YANWORTH 2½

COMPTON ABDALE 1½

CHEDWORTH 2
CIRENCESTER 8

MIND THE SNAILS!

Meet Chedworth's wildlife superstar: *Helix pomatia,* better known as the Roman snail. The Romans brought these snails with them for food, and their descendants are still living around the villa 1,500 years later. They're protected by law because they're so rare – Roman snails are only found on a few sites in the south of England. A recent study at Chedworth found at least 400 Roman snails living there, and they can live for as long as 20 years!

ROMAN WILDLIFE

As the name suggests, Roman snails were brought to Chedworth by the Romans. They also brought other species to Britain for food, like rabbits and even edible dormice. The dormice mostly died out after the Roman period and were re-introduced later.

The forests of Britain were scarier in Roman times. You could meet a wild boar or even a wolf amongst the trees. Brown bears still wandered around northern Britain too. Hunting expeditions were dangerous!

CONSERVATION

Roman snails are so rare that you need a special licence just to touch them. The National Trust rangers who look after Chedworth also have to look after the snails. In 2011 there was building work on site. Each Monday morning before the builders started work, the ranger went round collecting snails and moved them far enough away so they couldn't get back during the week.

ROMAN SNAILS LIKE ME PREFER TO LIVE IN PLACES WITH CHALK OR LIMESTONE IN THE SOIL. WE MAY NEED TO EAT CHALKY FOOD TO GROW OUR STRONG SHELLS.

A SPOTTER'S GUIDE

As well as snails, visitors to Chedworth may be able to spot rare birds like the marsh tit or the goldcrest. If you're at Chedworth around dusk, keep an eye out for a dark shape flying by with a jerkier movement than a bird. It could be a barbastelle bat, which is one of the rarest mammals in Britain.

MAKE YOUR OWN HIBERNACULUM

If you have access to a garden, you could build a hibernaculum – it will help all sorts of wildlife, from spiders and bugs to newts and lizards, and would provide a cosy home for snails to hibernate in over winter.

✓ Collect rocks, sticks, and maybe bits of old brick, and pile them up loosely, making sure there's space in between for creatures to curl up.

✓ To make sure animals can get in, stick in passages made of bits of drainpipe; if your pipes are plastic, scrape the insides with sandpaper so the animals can grip the sides, and add old leaves.

✓ Pile soil on top of the hibernaculum, and if you like, plant grass or wild flowers on top.

QUIZ: TEST YOUR KNOWLEDGE OF ROMAN BRITAIN!

1. About how long did the Roman army spend in Britain?

A. 50 years
B. more than 350 years
C. 600 years
(p2)

2. Which queen led a rebellion against the Romans in the year 60?

A. Cleopatra
B. Victoria
C. Boudicca
(p2)